My Dog Bit My Book!

By Cameron Macintosh

All the kids at school had to make a little book.

Bren would make a book on cats.

Bren spent a long time
on his book.

"It's very good!" said Dad.

But just then, Cookie the dog
chomped on Bren's book!

Bren pulled, and Cookie pulled.

Cookie shook the book
from side to side.

Bren put his foot on Cookie and pushed!

Cookie bit the book in two!

"Oh no!" said Bren.

He put the bits of book in his bag.

At school, Bren's friend Dong-Wook stood up.

"Look at my book on slugs!" he said.

"Very good, Dong-Wook!" said Miss Hay.

Then, Bren's friend Nat
stood up.

"Look at my book on the bush!"
she said.

"It looks great, Nat!"
said Miss Hay.

Then, Miss Hay said,
"Where is your book, Bren?"

"My dog Cookie bit my book,"
said Bren.

Bren took the bits of his book out of his bag.

"Your dog **did** bite your book!" said Miss Hay.

"Cookie does not like cats," said Bren.

"We can put the bits
of your book on this card,"
said Miss Hay.

"It's a stiff book, but it looks good," said Bren.

"Cookie will **not** rip this book!" said Miss Hay.

CHECKING FOR MEANING

1. How did Bren try to get his book back from Cookie? *(Literal)*

2. What did Dong-Wook write a book about? *(Literal)*

3. How do you think Bren felt when Cookie bit his book? *(Inferential)*

EXTENDING VOCABULARY

school	What is a *school*? Are all schools the same? What would you expect to find at most schools?
spent	Look at the word *spent*. What does the word *spent* mean? Explain that *spent* can mean 'used up', i.e. in the story, Bren spent a lot of time making his book.
chomped	What word with a similar meaning to *chomped* did the author also use in this book? What other words with a similar meaning could have been used?

MOVING BEYOND THE TEXT

1. If you had to write a book, what topic would you choose? Why?

2. What can dog owners do to make sure their pets do not bite items such as books?

3. Who was your favourite character in this book? Why?

4. What other excuses do people give for not handing in their homework?

DIPHTHONGS

| oy | ow | oo | aw |

PRACTICE WORDS

book

good

school

stood

Cookie

shook

Dong-Wook

Look

looks

pushed

took

pulled

foot

bush

put